11/18
946.08 Bye

TECH IN THE TRENCHES

Strategic Inventions of the Spanish Civil War

Ann Byers

Cavendish Square

New York

Published in 2017 by Cavendish Square Publishing, LLC
243 5th Avenue, Suite 136, New York, NY 10016

Library of Congress Cataloging-in-Publication Data

Names: Byers, Ann.
Title: Strategic inventions of the Spanish Civil War / Ann Byers.
Description: New York : Cavendish Square Publishing, 2017.
| Series: Tech in the trenches | Includes index.
Identifiers: ISBN 9781502623553 (library bound) | ISBN 9781502623560 (ebook)
Subjects: LCSH: Spain--History--Civil War, 1936-1939. | Spain-
-History--Civil War, 1936-1939--Technology.
Classification: LCC DP269.B94 2017 | DDC 946.081--dc23

Editorial Director: David McNamara
Editor: Kristen Susienka
Copy Editor: Nathan Heidelberger
Associate Art Director: Amy Greenan
Designer: Jessica Nevins
Production Coordinator: Karol Szymczuk
Photo Researcher: J8 Media

The photographs in this book are used by permission and through the courtesy of: Cover U.S. Air
Force photo/Staff Sgt. Aaron Allmon/Wikimedia Commons; p. 4 Photo 12/Contributor/Getty
Images Entertainment/Getty Images; p. 11 Hulton Archive/Stringer/Getty Images Entertainment/
Getty Images; p. 14 Universal History Archive/Contributor/Getty Images Entertainment/Getty
Images; p. 20 conejota (/gallery-1711990p1.html)/Shutterstock; p. 25 Mariano Benlliure y Gil/
Wikimedia Commons; p. 28 World History Archive/Alamy Stock Photo; p. 30 Phil Crean A/
Alamy Stock Photo; p. 34 NordNordWest/Modifications by user: Sting, Grandiose/Wikimedia
Commons; p. 39 ullstein bild/Contributor/Getty Images Entertainment/Getty Images; p. 40
Universal History Archive/Contributor/Getty Images Entertainment/Getty Images; p. 44
Этоизображение (илидругоймедиафайл) находится в общественном достоянии (англ.
public domain), так как его авторское право истекло./Wikimedia Commons; p. 44 Flavio
Mucia (AMB Brescia)/Wikimedia Commons; p. 49 http://www-af.mil (PD-USGov-Military-Air
Force)/Wikimedia Commons; p. 53 ullstein bild/Contributor/Getty Images Entertainment/Getty
Images; p. 54 Mikhail Koltsov/Wikimedia Commons; p. 61 Daily Herald Archive/Contributor/
Getty Images Entertainment/Getty Images; p. 64 El noi de la garriga/Wikimedia Commons; p. 72
World History Archive/Alamy Stock Photo; p. 74 Sueddeutsche Zeitung Photo/Alamy Stock
Photo; p. 81 World History Archives/Alamy Stock Photo; p. 83 Sueddeutsche Zeitung Photo/
Alamy Stock Photo; p. 86 Fine Art/Contributor/Getty Images Entertainment/Getty Images;
p. 88 SeM/Contributor/Getty Images Entertainment/Getty Images; p. 93 Fox Photos/Stringer/
Getty Images Entertainment/Getty Images; p. 97 AFP/Stringer/Getty Images Entertainment/
Getty Images; BRU GARCIA/Stringer/Getty Images Entertainment/Getty Images.

Printed in the United States of America

CONTENTS

French men and women line up to receive food in 1932, during the Great Depression. The woman helping distribute the packages is Josephine Baker, an American-born singer and dancer extremely popular in France.

Europe Between the Wars

The 1920s and 1930s were difficult everywhere, but especially in Europe. The Great War, which later became known as World War I, ended in 1918, leaving destruction, disillusionment, and chaos in its wake. It had erased or moved national borders, emptied treasuries, and practically wiped out a generation of men. Between the two world wars, Europe was awash in political, economic, and social turmoil.

POLITICAL UPHEAVAL

After the Great War, four empires that had dominated the continent for centuries were no more. When Germany lost the war, the emperor, Kaiser Wilhelm II, gave up his throne, and the winners took bits of Germany's territory for themselves. A large chunk was cut away and given to Poland.

The massive Austro-Hungarian Empire had splintered into several smaller nations in the waning days of the war. Czechoslovakia and Poland broke away and became **sovereign** states. Slovenia, Bosnia, and Croatia declared themselves independent of the empire and soon merged with Serbia and other small groups to form Yugoslavia. Hungary and Austria, each reduced to a fraction of its former size, were divided into two separate countries.

To the east, Russia was in the **throes** of revolution and civil war. Territories on the northwestern edge of the vast Russian Empire— Finland, Estonia, Latvia, and Lithuania—pulled away. In the southwest, fighting raged in Turkey, Romania, Ukraine, Belarus, Armenia, and other areas.

The Ottoman Empire, which once stretched across the Middle East, over northern Africa, and into eastern Europe, had begun to disintegrate long before the war. The weakened empire allied itself with Germany and thus was on the losing side. Turkey won its independence, but England and France took over the rest of the empire and divided it between them, governing the different parts like colonies.

When the map of Europe was redrawn, some of the boundary lines did not make sense. People who felt they belonged together found themselves in different countries. Millions of Hungarians were now in Slovenia, Romania, and Yugoslavia. German-speaking people were scattered among several of the new states. New borders separated tribal groups throughout the Middle East. Many people became minorities overnight in what had been their own lands.

The nations that emerged from the shambles of World War I had been monarchies. Whether the ruler was called a king, a kaiser, a czar, or an emperor, he had absolute control. The common people did not vote; decisions were made by the monarch and a small group of nobles. In the new order, there would be no kings to tell the people what to do, to settle disputes, to build roads and bridges, and to keep them safe. Without any experience in **democracy**, the people would have to figure out how to govern themselves. This made the interwar period a time of political floundering for much of Europe.

ECONOMIC RUIN

The political crisis was made worse by economic disaster. The war had cost more than $200 billion, money spent on tanks, bombs, and other weaponry that was now utterly destroyed or no longer of any use. The harsh terms of the Treaty of Versailles saddled Germany with a crippling debt. Nations—winners and losers alike—were not merely bankrupt; they owed huge sums. Some of the money was owed to their citizens, who had bought bonds to finance the war. Much was owed to the United States.

The governments did not have the means to repay the massive amounts they had borrowed. Manufacturing, trade, and even agriculture had been disrupted by the fighting and could not be restored easily. The war had claimed the lives of nine million servicemen and five million civilians, people who would not return to the factories and the fields. In the last year of the conflict and for two full years after, one of the worst flu epidemics in history swept the entire globe, killing more than fifty million and crushing what little economic life there was.

Just as a glimmer of recovery was beginning to appear, the stock market crash of 1929 plunged the world into economic depression. Banks failed, prices skyrocketed, and the value of currency plummeted. Those who had jobs lost them, and poverty stalked every city. Throughout Europe, the interwar period was a time of economic desolation.

SOCIAL UNREST

The political and economic instability shook the people of Europe to their core. They had gone into the conflict proud and optimistic, but four years of carnage and deprivation left them stunned and empty. The downfall of monarchies meant an upending of the social order, a shuffling of power and positions. Everything people had depended on had failed them. They had enjoyed decades of peace, but now they feared war could erupt at any minute. They had been prosperous, or at least comfortable, but in the 1920s and 1930s, people begged in the streets. The horrible devastation of the war shattered their faith in government, employers, bankers, and rulers.

The frustration and disillusionment led to anger. The people directed their anger at the institutions and leaders they could no longer trust. Factory workers went on strike, soldiers **mutinied**, unemployed men rioted. The disputes and demonstrations frequently turned violent. Socially, the interwar period was unsettled.

All over Europe, people looked for solutions. They knew they could never put their world back together the way it was; they needed some new order. Two **ideologies** appeared in those confused years, two ways of looking at and fixing the political, economic, and social havoc. The two systems of thought were socialism and fascism.

CONFLICTING SOLUTIONS

Socialism is based on the idea that everything should be fair and equal. All people have the same value, so no one should have more than anyone else. In its extreme form, communism, no one owns anything; everything belongs to everybody. Some people will naturally make more money than others because their land is richer, they are stronger, or for whatever reason. To keep everyone equal, their "extra" needs to be taken from them and given to those who do not have as much. Who decides how much is extra? The only way to distribute a country's resources and products fairly is for someone, typically the government, to take charge of everything.

Under fascism also, the government—often called the "state"— controls everything. Fascism can be defined as a government system in which the state controls the economy, the political structures, and the media. Individuals own their own property and businesses, but the state tells them what they can and cannot do with their possessions. Unlike socialism, which proclaims that all people are equal, fascism has very strict classes. For example, Nazism was a form of fascism, and in Nazi Germany, the state declared that some people were so low in the social hierarchy that they were not even worthy of life.

The two philosophies are very different in many ways. Socialism is a bottom-up theory: the people rule. Fascism is top down: a dictator makes all decisions. Socialism has an international outlook; the communist slogan at the time was "Workers of the world, unite!" Fascism is extremely nationalistic, demanding loyalty to one's country. Because socialism originally sought radical social change, it was called a left-wing, or liberal, philosophy. Fascism, which kept, or conserved, some of the traditional elements of society, was considered right-wing, or conservative. (The terms "left wing" and "right wing" originated from the seating of liberals and conservatives in the French National Assembly during the French Revolution.)

Despite their differences, in actual practice the two political systems in their extreme forms have much in common. For instance, both reject democracy and capitalism. Although communism preaches rule by the people, a dictatorial leader often emerges, so both systems are **authoritarian**, meaning that political authority rests in one person or one small group. In both communism and fascism, the government runs everything and makes all decisions. The state monitors all forms of communication: news, education, entertainment. The leaders maintain control through terror and violence.

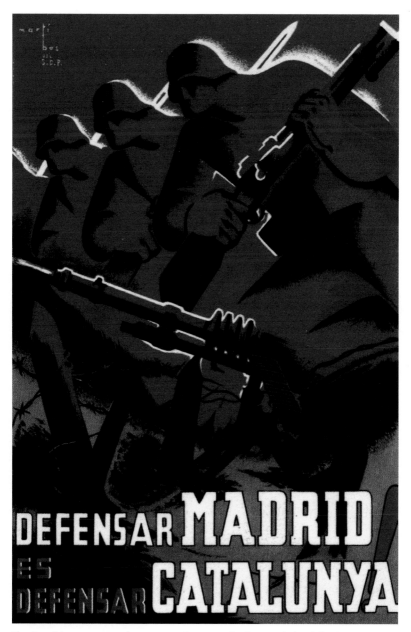

This Republican propaganda poster proclaims, "Defending Madrid is defending Catalonia." Its artist attempted to rally Spaniards in Madrid and Catalonia to unite to defeat the Nationalists.

To some Europeans wary of oppressive rulers, the socialist concept of a classless society was appealing. Workers who had always been poor liked the idea of redistributing wealth. Others, eager to restore their countries' honor, were drawn to the militaristic nationalism of fascism. Many, with no experience in democracy, looked for strong leaders to bring them out of the chaos and gloom left by the Great War. By 1933, Russia had embraced communism, and Italy and Germany had both become fascist.

SPAIN BETWEEN THE WARS

The decision about what form of government to adopt took longer in Spain. Spain had been neutral in the war, but its citizens suffered the same devastating effects as the rest of Europe. The Great Depression and the worldwide flu epidemic took heavy tolls on the entire continent. High prices, food shortages, and unemployment plagued Spain almost as severely as the countries that fought. Riots and strikes added to the distress.

The country's leaders were completely incapable of bringing stability or prosperity to their people. In the first five years after the war, Spain seesawed between twelve different governments; none was able to calm the nation's fears and discontent. With each new administration, anger rose and positions hardened. The tension finally exploded in 1936 in a full-scale civil war.

The Spanish Civil War pitted the left against the right, communists and socialists against fascists. At the time, many saw it as a struggle for civilization against extreme political philosophies; tens of thousands came from fifty countries to fight on one side or the other. The conflict lasted three years, from July 1936 to April 1939, and claimed the lives of five hundred thousand people. It was one of the bloodiest chapters in Spain's history.

The Spanish Civil War is sometimes called the **prelude**, or opening act, to World War II. During the war, some of the alliances for the later conflict were cemented. More importantly, Germany was able to create and test in Spain some of the air combat tactics and technologies it would use to deadly effect in the next war. New fighter plane formations, bombing strategies, and military aircraft were developed during the Spanish Civil War. In contrast to its value as the proving grounds for deadly technologies, the conflict also became a laboratory for life-saving medical innovation. New methods of wound care and of collecting and storing blood were pioneered in Spain. The technologies developed during the Spanish Civil War make this brief event sandwiched between two world wars one of the most important conflicts of modern times.

Most of the farms in Spain were large estates called *latifundios*, and most of the farm work was done by hand or by animals.

CHAPTER
ONE

Spain in the Early 1900s: Divided and Volatile

ong before World War I plunged Europe into turmoil, Spain was already in political and social disarray. In fact, the history of Spain for more than a century was riddled with riots and revolts, assassinations and abdications, military takeovers and civil wars. From 1814 to 1874, twelve **coups** rocked the government. The political turbulence was fed by three structures that were behind the times: an economy that was woefully weak, a religion that was overly strong, and a military that could not perform.

A BACKWARDS ECONOMY

Spain entered the twentieth century somewhat behind most of Europe. The Industrial Revolution that had brought prosperity to other nations was late in coming to Spain. With very little manufacturing, Spain's economy was primarily agricultural; two-thirds of the population was employed in farming. However, the land was not particularly suitable for growing crops. The terrain was rough, the soil poor, and rainfall scarce.

Farming was especially difficult in the northern region. Here, some individuals had tiny plots of ground that produced very little. Most lived on the edge of starvation. The land in the central and southern parts of the country was better, but the people who worked there did not own the land they farmed. Rather, in a holdover of the feudalism of medieval times, a few privileged people owned large estates, meaning the bulk of all property in Spain belonged to a handful of rich people. The lopsided distribution of land created two social classes: a very small aristocracy of extremely wealthy landowners and a very large underclass of poor laborers and landless peasants.

In poor countries, such as Spain was, money often equals power. The landowners controlled not only their estates but also the government. The poor had no voice in political matters and no way to improve their lot.

A POLITICAL CHURCH

Landowners were not the only rich people in Spain in the early twentieth century. The **clergy** of the Catholic Church had great wealth, power, and influence. The Catholic Church was a firmly entrenched part of Spanish life. Throughout much of the country's history, its rulers had called themselves the "Catholic monarchs of Spain." They had succeeded in forcing all Muslims and all Jews out of the country. Spain's rulers had seen themselves and their nation as the world's defenders of the Catholic faith. By law, Catholicism had been the official religion of Spain since 1851.

As a result, the Catholic Church and the government had become closely intertwined. Church leaders were selected from the landed aristocracy. The government paid the salaries of priests and bishops and decided who would be appointed to the most well paid and most influential offices. In return, religious officials supported political leaders and called on their congregations to do the same. The Catholic Church was placed in charge of the nation's entire education system, so it controlled moral, social, and political thought. Much of that thought was stuck in the past, ignoring new ideas that were overtaking the rest of Europe.

AN OUT-OF-DATE MILITARY

Perhaps the social and political force most stubbornly mired in the past was the military. For centuries, the military had been the pride of Spain. It had built and maintained one of the largest empires in history. However, several decades of steady decline had sapped it of its glory. The final jolt to its honor was a surprise military rout the country called the "Disaster." In the Spanish-American War of 1898, Spain was soundly defeated by the young United States. The Disaster stripped the country of the last of its overseas possessions and left it humiliated and impoverished. It also demoralized the soldiers and stirred public opposition to the army.

The people saw the military as a completely ineffective relic of an earlier time. No longer able to hold onto an empire, it was being used to quell discontent at home. In the 1800s, the army put down revolts and fought five civil wars. Its brutal methods further inflamed the people against the military.

In addition to its incompetence, the army was expensive. It was large and top-heavy with officers, most from the upper class of landowners. The ratio of officers to soldiers was about one to six. The common people resented the bite the military took of their taxes. They also resented the fact that the unpopular officers wielded considerable power. The generals saw themselves as the protectors of the nation, and anytime a political crisis threatened, they swept in and presented themselves as saviors.

THE RESTORATION

That is exactly what happened in 1874. An army officer ended the First Spanish Republic, which had lasted less than a year, and reinstated the monarchy. This began a period known as the Restoration. The new order was a **parliamentary** government; the king, Alfonso XII, shared power with a legislature called the Cortes. The Cortes created a constitution in 1876 that spelled out how the system would operate.

After so many government upheavals, the Cortes was determined to write a constitution that would bring stability to the country. The instability had come from power struggles between two political parties: the Conservatives and the Liberals. Generally speaking, the Conservative Party favored the status quo—that is, wanted to keep things as they were—and the Liberal Party wished to institute a few reforms such as permitting the press greater freedom and allowing more people to vote. In reality, however, there was little difference between the parties at that time. Both were composed of the wealthy and powerful, and neither was willing to give up its wealth and power.

To avoid conflict, the Cortes devised the *turno pacifico* system. Literally "peaceful turnaround," turno pacifico meant that the two parties would take turns controlling the Cortes. The king would appoint a prime minister from one party and most of the members of the Cortes would be from that party during his turn. After a few years, the king would appoint a prime minister from the other party. The system appeared democratic—that is, most men could vote for representatives in the Cortes. However, the only way the arrangement could work was for the government to rig the elections. Widespread use of intimidation and outright fraud enabled the ruling classes to maintain their shared power and silence all voices except those of the two approved parties.

Despite its flaws, the 1876 constitution ushered in almost fifty years of relative political stability—somewhat of a record for Spain. The calm permitted economic growth. Industry finally sprouted and a middle class began to grow. However, although the government was reasonably stable during the Restoration, society was not. Discontent continued to fester among the people. Prosperity created new forces that were not happy with the status quo and were increasingly willing to express their dissatisfaction.

PRESSURES FOR CHANGE

One of the forces challenging the Restoration was a growing restlessness in the north of Spain, particularly in the region of Catalonia and the Basque provinces. Many in these areas wanted to separate themselves from the monarchy. They were distinct from other Spaniards ethnically; they had their own languages and customs. Catalans and Basques did not believe the central government in Madrid represented them or protected their

To this day, many Catalans and Basques continue to call for separation from Spain. This 2015 photo shows a Catalan independence demonstration in Barcelona on September 11, Catalonia's National Day.

interests. They pushed for independence, or at least more political power for their regions.

These areas had been the first to industrialize, as early as the 1840s. Catalonia had textile factories, and the Basques operated iron and steel mills. The industrialization gave rise to a middle class, large cities, and movement of people from rural to urban areas. Unpleasant conditions in the factories led to labor movements. At first, workers simply reacted spontaneously to disagreeable situations in mills or mines by going on strikes or rampages to protest what they considered unjust treatment. Over time, however, the work stoppages became more organized and eventually mushroomed into large, full-fledged movements. They were not limited to factories or industrial centers; peasants on farms in Andalusia formed unions and made their complaints heard.

The different workers' groups put pressure on the government for different goals. Peasants wanted to see an end to large estates and a redistribution of land. Socialists agitated for economic and political power for laborers. Anarchists pushed for a society without government, a world in which order comes from people's voluntary cooperation. These movements were not unique to Spain; the same kinds of thinking had become popular in other parts of Europe.

POLITICAL PARTIES

The labor movements and trade unions were the basis of new liberal political parties. Unlike the older Liberal Party, which was part of the government, these new groups challenged the ruling

The Tragic Week

Barcelona in 1909 was a polarized city. At one end were the rich: Catholic clergy and industrialists who owned cotton, iron, and cork businesses. At the other end were the poor: workers who labored long hours in the factories of the wealthy. In this, the largest city in Catalonia, anger seethed barely beneath the surface and erupted at any provocation. The government presented a major provocation in July 1909.

Spain needed soldiers for its unpopular war in Morocco. The prime minister called reservists—men who had already completed their military duty—from Catalonia to serve in the army. They were all from the working class; people with money could pay for others to take their places. Anarchist and socialist leaders rallied distraught citizens to protest by refusing to work.

On July 26, factories in Barcelona were shut down and stores did not open. The strike spread to other Catalan cities. Not content with peaceful demonstrations, the people turned their pent-up anger toward Catholic institutions, burning eighty buildings and digging up graves. Officers ordered the army to stop the violence, but the soldiers refused to shoot their fellow Catalans. The government had to bring soldiers from other provinces to crush the revolt.

In what has been called the "Tragic Week," more than 100 civilians were killed, and over 1,700 were imprisoned. The event cemented the influence of anarchists in Catalonia; when an anarchist trade union was formed in 1911, 80 percent of Barcelona's workers joined. In the fourteen years following the Tragic Week, eight hundred strikes paralyzed the city.

class. They were made up largely of working people who wanted more than small reforms; they envisioned radical changes in the way the government operated. In addition to anarchist and socialist parties, there was another liberal group, the Republican Party. Republicans called for doing away with the monarchy altogether, replacing it with a representative form of government, a republic. As the liberal groups grew larger and louder, the country appeared to be splitting into two camps. On one side were the liberals; on the other was the Conservative Party, committed to preserving the monarchy and the corrupt system that propped it up. The two factions became more clearly defined during World War I.

Spain was neutral in the conflict, but Spaniards took sides. Many of them saw the war as a contest between conservatism and liberalism. To Spaniards of the Restoration period, conservatism, represented by Germany and the Central powers, meant the existing order: monarchy, aristocracy, Catholicism, and rigid control by a central government. Liberalism, championed by France and other Allies, meant a new order: democracy, secularism, and a reallocation of land and wealth. During the war, the conservatives in Spain were called "germanophiles" (literally, "lovers of Germany"). In this group were the large landowners, the clergy, and the army. Those on the liberal side, called "francophiles" because they were pro-France, were the anarchists, socialists, and Republicans. Catalans, Basques, and others who wanted regional independence were also francophiles. By the end of the war, most Spaniards were on one side or the other.

World War I brought prosperity to Spain as countries on both sides bought Spanish goods. The fledgling industries of the northern regions expanded, and the agricultural estates in the south sent their produce abroad. But the prosperity was short lived. Spain could not keep up with the demand, and exporting products to other countries created shortages at home. Prices rose and working conditions deteriorated. The economic gains went to those who were already wealthy—the landholders and business owners—and the hardships fell on the masses of workers and peasants. The divide between rich and poor widened.

PRIMO DE RIVERA

People were frustrated with the government's inability to solve the domestic problems. Adding to that frustration was exasperation over a protracted war in Africa. Spain held a small sliver of land in Morocco. It was of little economic value to Spain, but it was important to the country's prestige and honor. After the Disaster of 1898, Spain was determined to hold on to its possession in Africa. The army was sent to "pacify," or gain control over, the tribes that lived there. The tribes resisted, and the result was a series of wars that dragged on from 1909 to 1927. The army blamed its heavy losses on the government's failure to supply it with adequate men, money, and equipment. The government accused the military of corruption and ineptness. The people at

A statue of Miguel Primo de Rivera stands in Jerez de la Fontera. The general was born into a wealthy family in Jerez, a city famous for breeding and training horses.

home blamed both; they staged protests, one that ended with over a hundred citizens killed.

These protests, as well as riots over food shortages, strikes against employers, and general unrest among workers, became increasingly frequent and violent. The country was ripe for a general to step in as savior. In 1923, Captain General Miguel Primo de Rivera staged a coup d'etat, an overthrow of the government.

Military coups in Spain were not like those in most other countries; they were often bloodless. They began when a general issued a *pronunciamiento*, an announcement of his criticisms of the government. If the majority of the army agreed with the general, the government resigned and the general took over. If the general did not have support, the coup failed. Most soldiers, having suffered a huge defeat in a war they did not want to fight, sided with Primo de Rivera. The king, Alfonso XIII, was forced to accept the coup and appoint Primo de Rivera prime minister.

Primo de Rivera was conservative. His coup, under the banner "Country, Religion, Monarchy," was backed by the three conservative elements of the country: landowners, the Catholic Church, and the army. He did not overthrow the king. Rather, he believed the politicians and a corrupt government system were responsible for the country's problems. So he did away with the system; he suspended the constitution, dissolved the Cortes, and ruled as a dictator.

The people were pleased with some of Primo de Rivera's initial actions. He improved Spain's road, rail, and power systems, and he ended the wars in Africa with a victory. But he angered Catalans by taking away some of their privileges, and he upset workers by allowing the army to stop labor demonstrations harshly. His work projects bankrupted the country, and all his support eventually crumbled. In 1930, Primo de Rivera resigned.

SECOND SPANISH REPUBLIC

No general came forward to save Spain. Instead, leaders of at least eight liberal political movements joined together and formed a new government. They held elections on April 12, 1931, and a majority voted for Republicans. Two days later, the victors proclaimed the beginning of the Second Spanish Republic. The king fled, leaving his country to the new, liberal regime.

The Republicans lost no time in making changes. They stripped landowners of their privileges, took education away from the Catholic Church, and began to correct abuses in the military. They gave Catalonia and the Basque provinces the right to govern themselves. These "reforms" pleased the left-leaning groups, but they angered many on the right.

As in the past, the various factions vied for power, and leaders fell in and out of favor. Twenty or more political parties were represented in the Cortes. Liberals made up the majority in 1931 because several leftist groups had joined together

As a huge crowd gathers to celebrate the proclamation of the Second Spanish Republic, its leaders raise a new flag to symbolize a new beginning.

Strategic Inventions of the Spanish Civil War

in a coalition, an alliance. In 1933, the liberal parties were split, and a conservative coalition won the election. The Conservatives—primarily the aristocracy, the Catholic Church, and military officers—set about undoing the gains the Liberals had made.

In the 1936 election, the roles were again reversed. Liberal groups united and won the majority of votes. By this time, the economic, social, and political turbulence of the country had reached fever pitch. It seemed time for a general to come to the rescue.

This monument on the Canary Island of Tenerife was erected in 1958 to mark the spot where Francisco Franco met with coconspirators on June 17, 1936. Neglected and defaced, it was demolished in November 2015.

A Country
Torn Apart

our generals presented themselves as Spain's saviors in
1936. All four were career military men, and all four had
seen service in the brutal wars in Morocco. They were decorated
heroes. Each one had been awarded at least one medal for bravery
on the battlefield. All had positions of honor and influence. But
all four were opposed to the actions of the liberal governments,
especially their attempts to reform the military. They spoke out
publicly against them.

Because they criticized those who came to power in 1936, the
generals were reassigned to less important posts. Shortly after the
elections in February, three of them—José Sanjurjo, Emilio Mola,
and Manuel Goded Llopis—began plotting to seize control of the
government. In order for their plot to succeed, they had to make

sure the most able military leaders were with them. Without a
strong army, the coup would fail. So these generals approached
one of the most well known of their ranks, a man named
Francisco Franco.

Franco did not support the plot at first. Despite his
unhappiness with the liberal regime, the general had a good career.
A fifth-generation military officer, he was the youngest general
in Europe. He had distinguished himself in Morocco, surviving
a gunshot wound and leading an army known for its fierceness.
When Spain built a new military academy, Franco was selected to
direct it. A failed coup could jeopardize his future. But after being
banished to an insignificant assignment in the Canary Islands, he
was willing to talk with the conspirators. By the beginning of July,
Franco was on board.

THE COUP

The coup was set for July 18. Franco prepared the
pronunciamiento, the declaration of complaints against the
political leaders. In it the general explained why the officers felt
justified in rebelling against the legitimately elected government.
He criticized the leaders for permitting "anarchy … revolutionary
strikes … serious crimes." He accused "a bungling central
government" of cooperating with foreign powers to destroy Spain.
As he called upon "the Army, the Navy, and forces of public order"
to rise up "to defend the Motherland," he promised they would do
so "without rancor [bitterness] or violence." But he also warned
that opposition would be met with brutality: "The force that will

be used to maintain order will be proportionate to the magnitude of the resistance encountered."

Before issuing the pronunciamiento, Franco was to fly to Morocco and assume command of Spain's Army of Africa. This thirty-thousand-man force was actually two armies: the Spanish Legion and the Regulares. The Regulares consisted of Moroccans, sometimes called Moors, led by Spanish officers. The Army of Africa was Spain's top military force—professional, battle hardened, fearless, and led by the best commanders. The plan was for soldiers stationed throughout the country to respond to the pronunciamiento by taking control of government structures. The troops in Morocco would have a head start. After securing Spain's possessions in Africa, they would be ferried across the strait to the mainland. There they would join the uprisings occurring simultaneously in every province. They would crush all opposition easily and the coup would be over in a matter of weeks, if not days.

However, all did not go as planned. Word of the revolt got out, and the Moroccan troops were forced to move the rebellion up a day. Franco had to make his proclamation by radio from the Canaries and then fly to Africa. There and in many places across Spain, soldiers rose up and took charge. But in most of the cities on the mainland, citizens resisted. They broke into military barracks, seized weapons, and fought the rebels in the streets. Political parties and trade unions formed militias—local armies— that defended their cities. Worse yet, only a small minority of the top army leaders and about half the other officers supported the rebellion. Many of the regular soldiers and most of the air force remained loyal to the government. In the navy, ships' crews refused to revolt and instead threw their commanders overboard.

After a week, the rebelling generals held only one-third of Spain. It was a sizable accomplishment, but it was far from what they had anticipated—and it was not "without rancor or violence." The coup had failed; the action was now a civil war.

In July 1936, immediately after the coup, the Nationalists controlled the areas in Spain in pink and the Republican government held on to the territory in blue.

Strategic Inventions of the Spanish Civil War

THE SIDES

Like most civil wars, the Spanish Civil War began as a rebellion. The generals tried to overthrow a government that had been elected in a democratic process. Before the revolt, Spain was splintered into many factions. The coup pushed groups together, dividing the country into two distinct blocs, one left-wing, the other right.

The two sides saw the conflict differently. Those on the left viewed it as a struggle between the working classes and the **elite**, between freedom and tyranny, between democracy and dictatorship, between a secular society and religious oppression. Those on the right presented it as a contest between anarchy and civilization. They saw themselves as fighting for traditional values—Catholicism, order, morality, discipline—against socialism and communism. Both groups were broad alliances and went by a number of names.

REPUBLICANS

The left-wing alliance was loyal to the government elected in February. Therefore, its members called themselves Loyalists. They were defending the republic against people who wanted to restore the monarchy, so they were also called Republicans. Believing they had the support of the majority of the populace, they called their forces the Popular Front. The word "front" means a partnership of different groups that unite for a common purpose.

The Popular Front was made up of liberals of all kinds: anarchists, socialists, and communists. It included people who were politically in the middle, who wanted some form of democracy; and radicals on the extreme left, who hoped to eventually overthrow all government. Radicals defended the government because it was closer to their goal than anything Spain had had so far. The working classes in the cities were Republicans, and so were most of the peasants. Educated people in the middle class, considering the liberal republic modern and the conservative monarchy backwards, were part of the Loyalist coalition. Catalans, Basques, and others who had experienced some independence under the republic also joined with the Popular Front. Because many of the groups in the front were communist, their enemies called them the Reds and their army the Red Horde.

NATIONALISTS

On the other side were the rebels. They, too, were a conglomeration of different interests. In addition to many generals, the landed aristocracy backed the revolt, as did businessmen, supporters of the monarchy, Catholic Church officials, and people opposed to communism. A fascist party called the Falange sided with the rebels. Fascism is an extreme right-wing ideology in which one person or group exercises tight control. Franco embraced this ideology and eventually outlawed all political parties except the fascist Falange. The rebels were called Fascists or The Falange. They were also known as insurgents because they surged up against the government, but the rebels called themselves Nationalists. That name suggested they represented the entire nation of Spain. But when the coup failed, the Nationalists had

A Forbidden Air Force

The Treaty of Versailles ending World War I was extremely harsh. It allowed Germany to keep only a very small army, hardly any navy, and absolutely no air force. Germany had to surrender all its planes, plane parts, and aviation equipment, and could not even make commercial airplanes or plane parts for six months.

But the country was determined to rebuild its military might despite being closely watched. Once the restriction was lifted, German companies started designing and manufacturing commercial planes. Some of the companies—Heinkel, Junkers, Dornier, Messerschmitt—built fighting aircraft as well, hiding them from the inspectors. As concealing the planes grew more difficult, Germany made a secret deal with the Soviet Union for use of a piece of land near Moscow. At this base in Fili, Hugo Junkers began manufacturing warplanes in 1922.

As Germany secretly accumulated a fleet of military aircraft, it needed skilled pilots to fly them. Training pilots in aerial combat was also forbidden to Germany. Again Germany turned to the Soviet Union. In exchange for providing the Soviet Air Force with its technical expertise, Germany was allowed to establish an operation in Lipetsk, 230 miles (370 kilometers) south of Moscow. What looked like a Soviet military base was in reality a flight training center for German aviators and a testing facility for German warplanes. One hundred twenty pilots were trained at this hidden location. Thus, by the time Hitler came to power, Germany had a large, modern, unofficial air force.

yet to gain control of the major cities; the industrial regions; and Madrid, the capital. And its main military force was still in Africa.

HELP FROM ABROAD

When Spain's sailors aligned themselves with the Republicans, they left the Army of Africa stranded in Morocco. The navy blockaded the Straits of Gibraltar, denying Franco passage to the mainland. Getting to the mainland was critical because the goal of the revolt was to capture Madrid. Franco's only option was to transport the army by air, but the Republicans possessed most of Spain's tiny air force. So Franco turned for help to the two right-wing governments in Europe, Fascist Italy and Nazi Germany.

Franco asked Adolf Hitler for ten airplanes to take his Army of Africa across the straits to Spain. Hitler weighed the pros and cons of supplying the insurgency. On the negative side, it could arouse the anger of England and France, and the Republicans might punish Germans living in Spain. But there were several pluses. If the rebels actually won, Hitler could have a right-wing ally that would enable him to box France in if he went to war. Germany was secretly preparing for war. Even if the revolt was not successful, a conflict in Spain would keep the world's attention off Germany and allow the war preparations to go undetected. In exchange for the planes, the rebels could supply Germany with iron ore, copper, and other minerals for making weapons. Hitler surprised Franco by giving him not ten but twenty planes. He called the airlift "Operation Magic Fire," a reference from a Wagner opera he had been watching when the request came.

The twenty planes were just the beginning of other countries' help for the Nationalists. In the three years of the civil war, Germany sent hundreds of planes, tons of bombs, many tanks, and nineteen thousand men. After Germany started supplying the rebels, Italy also came to their aid. Great Britain and France refused to get involved, but the Soviet Union supplied massive amounts of air power and personnel to the Republicans. Aside from any government help, more than thirty-five thousand people from fifty-two countries volunteered on the side of the Republicans. In an attempt to preserve democracy against a fascist threat, they formed military units known as the International Brigades. Thus the Spanish Civil War grew into a mini world war fought on a very small plot of ground.

Moroccan Regulares wait for the German Ju-52s to take them to the Spanish mainland.

Americans in the Fight

Like people from dozens of countries, Americans were drawn into the civil war raging in Spain. Young people in particular were attracted to the fight against fascism, many of them members of the American Communist Party. About 2,800 Americans volunteered to defend the Spanish Republic. They were from all walks of life—laborers and

Volunteers leave New York with high hopes to join the International Brigades.

lawyers, artists and athletes, professors and students. Some were veterans of World War I, but most were completely untrained for combat; many had never held a gun. The three American battalions (a battalion consists of three hundred to eight hundred soldiers) are often lumped together under the name the Abraham Lincoln Brigade (three to six battalions make a brigade). They were placed with three other battalions to form the Fifteenth International Brigade.

The American units were racially integrated at a time when the US Army was still segregated. One of the battalions was commanded by an African American named Oliver Law.

The United States government did not approve of the brigade because America had chosen to remain neutral in the war. Some of the volunteers found their passports stamped "not valid for travel to Spain," but they managed to get there. The International Brigades were often used as shock troops, launching sudden attacks on the enemy. This placed them on the front lines of some of the fiercest battles of the war. More than one-third did not return home.

Another 125 Americans volunteered in Spain with the American Medical Bureau. The bureau formed teams of doctors, nurses, and medical technicians that treated Republican soldiers. These brave Americans helped develop and implement new life-saving medical technologies.

BADAJOZ: PATTERN OF THE REVOLT

By the first week of August, most of the Army of Africa, along with its commander, Francisco Franco, was in Spain. By then, Mola and other Nationalist generals had claimed a good deal of territory for the insurgents. However, Mola's forces in the north were separated from those in the south by Extremadura, an area along the border with Portugal. When Franco arrived on the mainland, he ordered the army assembling in Seville to march north, capture the provinces of Extremadura, and unite the two Nationalist-held sections of the country. The first major battle of the Civil War was for the Extremadura province of Badajoz.

Badajoz was a rural area with little ability to withstand a professional military assault. The Republican Army had been slow to mobilize and was stretched thin by uprisings in multiple locations. Only five hundred soldiers were available to defend the main city in the region; the people had to rely on a hastily assembled militia of peasants with no military training and very few weapons. It was no match for the disciplined, heavily armed soldiers coming against it.

By August 10, the Nationalist troops had taken the other cities of Extremadura and were at the outskirts of Badajoz. For three days before the actual battle, the city was pummeled with **artillery** shells from the ground and bombs from the sky. The German planes that had airlifted Franco's troops from Morocco, now converted to bombers, flew almost nonstop over the city. In the brief intervals between bombings, when the terrified peasants came out of their hiding places, Hitler's fighter planes descended, **strafing** soldiers and civilians alike.

On August 14, the Nationalist Army stormed into the city in armored vehicles and on foot. Resistance was fierce but futile; the defenders were horribly outmanned and outgunned. The rebels were merciless; they killed even those who dropped their weapons and surrendered.

The slaughter did not end when the battle was over. For days afterward, the victorious soldiers rampaged through Badajoz, abusing and killing men and women. Citizens were herded by the hundreds into the local bullring and executed by machine gun. Most historians put the number of people killed in the province at between four thousand and six thousand. Franco denied the stories of the massacre, claiming they were propaganda spread by the Republicans; he insisted the Loyalists had set fire to the city. But before the Nationalists stormed Basque cities several days later, they dropped leaflets calling for surrender and threatening to do to those cities what they had done to Badajoz.

Badajoz was the Nationalists' first major victory, and it set the pattern for most of the fighting that was to follow. Cities would be attacked, and civilians would be considered valid targets. Populations would be terrorized before troops closed in, frightened into submission by days of bombing. Rather than taken prisoner, survivors would be executed. Atrocities on one side would be avenged by worse atrocities on the other. The death toll would be staggering. Reality would be twisted. Sadly, this pattern was made all the more severe by some of the technological innovations that came out of this war.

Several countries used the planes tested in the Spanish Civil War. The Russian Polikarpov I-16 (*top*) was given or sold to China, and the German Heinkel He-51 (*bottom*) belonged to Bulgaria.

Fighting
in the Air

At the time of the Battle of Badajoz, Francisco Franco was neither the leader of the rebellion nor the senior commander of the army. He was simply one of the plotters and head of one part of the military. But Sanjurjo had been killed in a plane crash, the coup had failed, and the revolt needed a leader. A group of generals met on September 21, 1936, and named Franco generalissimo, or commander in chief. A few days later, on October 1, the insurgents declared Nationalist Spain the rightful government and Franco *el caudillo*, the country's leader. Now it was up to the generalissimo to subdue the militias, the authorities, and the citizens who did not want him to lead them.

For that he would need more military equipment; all he had was what he could take from the Republican forces and what

Germany and Italy had given him. Spain's armaments were outdated and in poor shape, but he had the twenty German Junkers (Ju-52s) that had brought his troops to the mainland; he used these as bombers. Hitler had also sent six Heinkel fighter planes (He-51s), each with two machine guns, to protect the Junkers, and twenty antiaircraft guns to shoot down Republican planes that threatened the transport aircraft. Italy had also contributed planes, tanks, and motorized vehicles. These gave the Nationalists a huge advantage.

The Republicans also had an advantage: $750 million in gold. The Loyalists, the rightful government of Spain, used two-thirds of its gold to purchase military equipment from the Soviet Union. By the time Franco was proclaimed caudillo of Nationalist Spain, more than sixty Soviet fighter planes and bombers were on their way to the Republic. Franco appealed to Hitler for more help.

THE CONDOR LEGION

That help came in the form of a full-scale military task force developed just for the conflict in Spain. Called the Condor Legion, it included resources from the German army (artillery, tanks, antiaircraft guns, and their operators), navy (ships, submarines, and their crews), and air force (bombing, fighting, **reconnaissance**, and transport planes, and their pilots and mechanics). By far the largest part of the Condor Legion consisted of the air combat squadrons. Command of the different parts of the legion was therefore placed under the **Luftwaffe**, the German air force. The legion itself, however, was entirely under the direction of Franco; the Nationalist leader gave the orders and the Germans carried them out. The director of the Luftwaffe, Hermann Göring, said the Spanish Civil War gave him a chance to test his young air force, to develop new machines, and try new tactics.

The legion had its first test in November 1936 in the skies over Madrid. Meeting stiff resistance in their attempt to take the capital, the rebels bombarded the city using five Ju-52s protected by nine He-51s. Suddenly, twenty-four fighter aircraft zoomed toward them. Most were biplanes—planes with two sets of wings—like the Heinkels, but six were Polikarpov I-16 monoplanes. This Soviet model was the fastest, most advanced fighter plane of the time. It could change course so quickly the Republicans called it the *Moska*, or fly, and the Nationalists called it a *rata*, meaning rat.

Condor Legion officers realized that the Soviet plane was superior to Germany's best aircraft. Clearly Germany needed better designs, especially if Hitler intended to launch a war in the near future. The commander of the Condor Legion pressed the Luftwaffe for faster planes. This demand spurred production of new models, including what would become Germany's most versatile and effective plane: the Messerschmitt Bf 109. The Bf 109 could outrace, outmaneuver, and outgun the Soviet Moskas. It could dart, climb, roll, and dive, all at breakneck speed. It could turn quickly and tightly. The small, light monoplane turned the tide in the air war. After the 109s were introduced, the Nationalists began to control the skies.

WORLD WAR I FIGHTER PLANE TACTICS

The tactics the Condor Legion pilots used were developed in World War I. In that conflict, aircraft were thought of in much the same way as ground troops. They were used mainly for reconnaissance and for shooting at targets on the battlefield. The planes flew in straight lines, just as troops marched. But airmen could not see and shout at one another as soldiers could. Early pilots had no radios, and visual contact was limited by clouds and position in the line. In addition, the straight line was difficult to defend. Pilots had to concentrate on what was in front of them and had no way to spot enemy planes approaching their sides or rear. A straight line was "easy pickings" for antiaircraft crews on the ground.

Pilots overcame these drawbacks with an arrangement called the "V" formation, or **vic**. In the vic, three planes flew close together, the leader in front and a wingman at each side and to the rear of the leader, forming the letter V. The tight configuration enabled the three pilots to communicate with hand signals and stay together even when visibility was poor. The main advantage of the vic formation was that it was both offensive and defensive. While the lead pilot attacked targets on the ground, each wingman, looking not just ahead but also toward the other two planes, could see and fire at an oncoming enemy in the air. By the end of World War I, the three-plane vic was the standard formation in the air forces of every country involved. The vic was the basic unit, and several vics could be combined to form squadrons.

Although use of the vic greatly improved air combat, it had a few problems. The closeness of the configuration often forced pilots to focus on avoiding crashing into one another rather than attacking or looking out for enemy aircraft. The need to keep three planes together limited what each could do. A new tactic was developed in Spain, quite by accident.

NEW PLANE, NEW TACTIC

It was the arrival of the Bf 109 that brought about the change. At first, the legion received very few of the high-performance craft. Werner Mölders, a young officer in the Condor Legion, found himself one day with only five—not even enough for two vics. Frustrated, Mölders split the five 109s into two units, in the

The F-15 Eagle, the US Air Force's fighter jet, introduced in 1972, continues to fly in the finger-four formation, as pictured here.

The Airsick Aviator

The man largely responsible for one of the most significant innovations in aerial combat almost didn't fly. Werner Mölders (1913–1941) dreamed of being a pilot, but flying made him sick. Doctors declared him unfit for aviation. However, the determined army cadet worked hard to overcome his motion sickness and became the most decorated of all Luftwaffe fighter pilots. From 1938 to 1941, he flew more than four hundred missions over Spain, France, Britain, and the Soviet Union. He surpassed the record of World War I ace Manfred von Richthofen, the Red Baron. The Red Baron had scored 80 kills (shoot-downs of enemy aircraft); Mölders's official tally was 115, and he probably had at least 30 more.

Although ruthless in the air, Mölders was a kind man loved and respected by those who knew him. The men under his command affectionately called him "Vati," meaning "Daddy." He was also a man of principles who was angry with the Nazi regime when he heard rumors of its inhumane treatment of so many people. He threatened to return his many medals if he found the rumors to be accurate. He may not have learned the truth as he died in 1941, before the worst of the Nazi killings came to light. The Spanish Civil War and World War II ace died in a plane crash—not as a pilot in a fighter aircraft, but as a passenger on his way to attend the funeral of a fellow airman.

process devising one of the most important and enduring tactical innovations in aerial combat: the **Rotte** and **Schwarm**.

The Rotte (German for "pair") was a two-plane configuration. It consisted of a leader and a wingman. The lead plane was piloted by the more skilled pilot; he was the one who did the fighting. The wingman's job was to protect the lead's rear. The wingman flew to one side and slightly behind his comrade. Each pilot scanned the sky ahead, focusing inward, toward the other. This enabled them to cover each other's blind spots. One usually flew higher than the other so each could see the sun; pilots often tried to surprise their opponents by attacking from the blinding glare of the sun.

The Rotte was the basic fighting unit, but it was only half of the innovation; the other half was the Schwarm. Two Rotten formed a Schwarm. The four-plane Schwarm mirrored the Rotte; in a Schwarm, the two Rotten were arranged the same way the two planes were positioned in the Rotte. The lead pair was in front and the second pair, like the wingman of the Rotte, was to one side and slightly behind the lead Rotte. The formation is also called the "finger four" because the placement of the planes, when viewed from above, appears like the positions at the ends of the extended fingertips of a human hand. The two Rotten of the Schwarm flew at different altitudes, giving the four pilots a more complete view of their surroundings and more room for each to maneuver in an attack.

The Rotte and Schwarm were possible only because of what was then a new technology: radio. By the 1930s, radios had become developed to the point where pilots could use them to talk with each other in flight. That ability permitted planes to travel in formation at greater distances from one another. Instead of flying nearly wingtip to wingtip as in the vic, planes in a Rotte were as far as 600 feet (183 meters), or about twenty wingspans, apart. The loose formation meant less worry about collisions and greater maneuverability and flexibility. In addition, planes that were spread over a wider area were harder for the enemy to detect than a group traveling together.

The Rotte and Schwarm proved to be an invaluable tactical innovation for the Condor Legion. As Germany pumped more and better 109s into Spain, legion pilots used these formations to retake the skies. That ability led to a defining strategy that shaped the way Germany would conduct warfare: the first step in every battle was to establish air superiority.

German fighter planes fly in formation over Spain in 1936.

The banner reads, "They shall not pass! The Fascists want to conquer Madrid. Madrid will be the tomb of the Fascists." Madrid kept the Fascists from taking the city for two and a half years.

Terror from the Skies

The new tactics for fighter aircraft were very important, but fighter planes were not the major weapons of the air war. The "big boys" were the bombers. Fighters were for defense; bombers were for offense. The primary purpose of the fighters—the Heinkels, the Moskas, the 109s, and others—was to keep the enemy's planes and defenses from thwarting their side's battle objectives. The fighters escorted other planes. Their machine guns were also used to disable antiaircraft batteries on the ground and strafe columns of soldiers. However, the real damage that allowed armies to take territory was inflicted by the bombers.

BOMBERS

Long before the Spanish Civil War, Germany had contracted with Dornier to supply bombers for its secret air force. But problems delayed development of the aircraft, so in 1934 the government ordered Junkers to redesign its Ju-52 for military use. The Ju-52 was a commercial plane, created to carry passengers and haul cargo. The company tweaked the design, installing bomb bays (compartments for holding explosives) and adding two machine guns. The new bombers doubled as transport planes. The Dornier planes turned out not to be effective, so the Ju-52, the plane that brought Franco's troops from Morocco at the start of the war, became the Luftwaffe's first bomber.

Nicknamed "Aunt Ju," the Junker was made to hold seventeen people. It was big and slow, flying at about 150 miles (241 km) per hour. This is why it had to have fighter escorts to fend off the Soviet Moskas and other planes that darted about quickly. It did not have **sights** that would enable its pilots to accurately identify targets, so it had to fly low to discharge its bombs. This made it an easy target from the ground and was the reason taking out the antiaircraft guns at the beginning of a battle was so important.

Unhappy with the Ju-52's performance, the Condor Legion requested better bombers. Since the Luftwaffe was using the Spanish Civil War to test new designs, it was happy to oblige. Three new planes arrived in Spain in early 1937: the Do-17 from Dornier, the Ju-86 from Junkers, and the He-111 from Heinkel. The He-111 proved to be the best of the three. It could carry a heavier load of bombs than the Aunt Ju, could fly higher and longer, and was faster than most fighter planes. A total of ninety-four Heinkel bombers were used in the conflict in Spain. Once they were put into service, the Ju-52 functioned less as a bomber and more frequently as a transport plane.

DIVE BOMBING

All these planes were conventional bombers—that is, they operated the same way bombers had in the past, in World War I. They simply flew over the enemy and dropped their explosives over a target to blow it up. In the Spanish Civil War, the Luftwaffe experimented with a new type of plane, a dive bomber.

The concept of dive bombing—descending on a target at an almost vertical angle at breakneck speed, dropping a deadly discharge, and rising nearly as rapidly and steeply as in the descent—was developed by the United States Navy. German World War I ace Ernst Udet, who had become a stunt pilot after the war, saw the navy's dive bomber at an air show in Cleveland, Ohio, in 1933. Udet was involved in building Germany's secret air force, and he was convinced this new plane was just what Germany needed. He bought two of the dive bombers for German manufacturers to study. The Luftwaffe held a competition to see which company would produce the best model. Junkers won with the Ju-87.

The Ju-87 was a *Sturzkampfflugzeug*, literally a "plunge-battle aircraft," commonly known as the Stuka. It has been described as looking like a menacing vulture, with wings that bend down

The Reluctant Industrialist

Hugo Junkers (1859–1935), whose name is associated with some of the most famous aircraft of the two world wars, never wanted to build warplanes. He was a mechanical engineer, a professor, and a staunch pacifist. He was also a prolific inventor, winning a gold medal at the 1893 Chicago World's Fair for his calorimeter. The professor founded the Junkers Appliance Company to manufacture heaters, stoves, and other products based on his inventions.

Junkers became interested in planes in 1909, at age fifty. He envisioned the new technology of aviation being used to carry passengers and goods great distances, bringing people from different nations together in peaceful pursuits. Shortly after the outbreak of World War I, he built the first successful all-metal plane, dubbed the "Sheet Metal Donkey." Impressed with the lighter weight and greater speed of the metal craft, the German government pressed him into service designing and producing planes for the military.

After the war, Junkers returned to commercial aviation. When Germany began building its secret air force in the 1920s, the country's leaders wanted Junkers to construct the planes. At first he refused. Eventually he gave in to the government pressure, building a Junkers plant in Fili, near Moscow. Here he manufactured fighter planes and bombers for both Germany and the Soviet Union.

In 1926, Germany withdrew its financial backing from the Fili factory, forcing Junkers to turn his company over to the government. Junkers had other businesses and owned patents to his inventions, but the government took those too when Hitler came to power. The man who reluctantly designed the planes that enabled the German air force to perform so stunningly in World War II died under house arrest on his seventy-sixth birthday.

and then up, like those of a seagull. Three were delivered to the Condor Legion to test their effectiveness at hitting their targets and panicking the enemy. The plane was remarkable at both. The Stuka pilot could locate a precise target from an altitude of 15,100 feet (4,602 m) and destroy it within minutes. He could dive at a 60- to 90-degree angle at about 400 miles (644 km) per hour and drop his bomb within 16 feet (5 m) of his target. As if the sight of a monstrous, heavily armed bird racing to the ground were not terrifying enough, technicians added sirens to the planes. Popularly called "Jericho trumpets," the sirens had propellers that turned in the wind created by the dive, terrifying their targets with their screams.

NEW TACTIC: TERROR BOMBING

The Stuka could be used as part of a tactic that appeared first in the Spanish Civil War. Terror bombing is a prolonged, heavy aerial attack on civilian populations. It is also called saturation bombing or carpet bombing because the bombs appear to cover the ground like a carpet.

The idea of terror bombing came not from the planning of military strategists but from the frustration of a single general. From the very beginning of the war, Francisco Franco's main objective was to capture Madrid. His Nationalist troops arrived at its outskirts in early November 1936. Coming fresh from their success at Badajoz, the soldiers expected to take the city easily. But the Loyalist army and the citizens of Madrid, reinforced by the International Brigades, held them off for more than a week. Thousands on both sides died in the seemingly unending series of attacks and counterattacks. An angry Franco determined to break the will of the defenders; he ordered the residential areas of the city bombed, all except the wealthy district, where Nationalist supporters might live. He reasoned that terrorized citizens would give up the fight.

For three days, waves of Ju-52s flew over Madrid in steady streams, pummeling homes and streets with explosives and **incendiary bombs**. The planes came day and night, guided in the dark by the fires of the earlier bombs. Hospitals were demolished; neighborhoods were reduced to rubble; and hundreds of people were killed, injured, and left homeless. Yet the terror bombing did not have the intended effect. Instead of demoralizing its victims, it ignited defiance. The people rallied to what became the battle cry of the Republicans: "*¡No pasarán!*"— "You shall not pass!" Despite the failure, five months later the Nationalists resorted to terror bombing again, this time in the unsuspecting city of Guernica.

The day after the bombing of Guernica, London *Times* correspondent George Steer
wrote that the town "was a horrible sight, flaming from end to end." Almost nothing was
left standing.

GUERNICA

Guernica was actually a small town rather than a city, housing about five thousand people. It was a Basque town in a region adamantly opposed to the Nationalists. The Basque people had long resisted right-wing attempts to bring them under its rule, and Guernica was one of the centers and symbols of Basque liberty. It had little, if any, military significance; a single weapons factory was located outside the city, and a stone bridge on the edge of the town might be used by Republican soldiers fleeing fighting in other areas. Nevertheless, the Condor Legion was ordered to attack Guernica.

April 26, 1937, was a market day, so the streets of the little town were full of people. At 4:30 in the afternoon, church bells rang out a warning; someone had spotted a single German plane flying low toward the city. Guernica had no planes and no antiaircraft guns, so the people crowded into *refugios*, refuges they had prepared in their cellars. The German pilot was apparently scouting the town. When he saw no defenses, he dropped his bombs not on the weapons factory or the bridge, but on the center of the town.

After the blast, when all was quiet, people emerged cautiously from their shelters to tend to the wounded and the damage. They were still in the streets fifteen minutes later when the real attack began. Wave after wave of bombers came in twenty-minute intervals. The first sorties unleashed explosives that ripped buildings apart. The next waves dropped incendiaries—tubes of molten metal that set fire to the wooden houses, businesses, hospitals, and churches. Each attack was followed by fighter planes whose machine gunners picked off anyone standing—men, women, and children, as well as cattle and sheep. The terror rained down nonstop until dark, for a total of more than three hours. Fires blazed for three days afterward. When it was over, the entire city lay in ruins. The Basque government said more than 1,600 people were killed in the bombing, but historians now believe the number is closer to 300. While all of Guernica was leveled, neither the weapons factory nor the stone bridge was harmed. The event made little difference to the outcome of the war, but it introduced the new tactic of terror bombing to a horrified world.

In a makeshift hospital in the cave near the Catalan village of La Bisbal de Falset, International Brigade doctors treated the wounded.

Saving
Lives

War is a strange affair. While captains and generals concentrate on destroying things and killing people, others work desperately at saving lives. Because the lives affected are so many, the injuries so serious, and the conditions of war so difficult, medical care in theaters of combat is often improvised. Shortages of materials and the pressures of time cause people to resort to unusual ways of trying to stop bleeding and prevent infection. Sometimes these unorthodox methods turn out to be surprisingly effective.

Wars have given rise to some wonderful medical discoveries and innovations that have become standard practice in civilian health care. The profession of nursing began in the Crimean War. The Red Cross was born from the terrible carnage of an Italian

War of Independence, and the Civil War in the United States marked the beginning of the American Red Cross. Ambulances were first used in the Napoleonic Wars, and the idea of professional emergency medical technicians for those ambulances did not occur until the conflict in Vietnam. The Vietnam War also gave doctors new wound adhesives, glues that hold skin together without stitches. New and better bandages and tourniquets were developed in the twenty-first-century war in Iraq. Triage, the system today's medical staff rely on to determine how serious a person's condition is and how quickly that person should be treated, was developed in wartime. Although penicillin had been discovered in 1928, it was little used until more than a decade later, when its value was shown in World War II. War is often the laboratory for technological innovation in medicine.

In combat, one of the greatest challenges facing those rendering aid is bleeding. People who lose large quantities of blood can often be saved if they are given fresh blood, but in the 1930s, fresh blood was in short supply in battle zones. In the Spanish Civil War, doctors found a way to transfuse blood into wounded soldiers and civilians, saving many lives.

BLOOD TRANSFUSION

At the outbreak of the Spanish Civil War, the science of blood transfusion was still quite new. It had begun with a few teams of doctors performing direct transfusions in the early 1900s. They cut through the skin of both donor and recipient and inserted tubing so blood could flow from one to the other over the course of two or three hours. The procedure was not only difficult and tedious; it also failed frequently because the blood clotted and the doctors did not understand the importance of blood typing. The facts that blood came in different types and that the types could not mix were not discovered until 1900 and not generally accepted in the medical community for another decade. When scientists discovered in 1914 that adding sodium citrate to blood prevented clotting, they were able to collect blood from donors, store it for up to four weeks, and infuse it indirectly with a syringe.

The discovery was just in time for World War I, but many in the medical profession were skeptical. At the beginning of that war, military doctors were still performing direct transfusion, but only in the rare instances when soldiers could be taken to hospitals. The injured were more commonly treated in field hospitals set up in tents near the front. In the last two years of the war, American and Canadian doctors brought portable blood transfusion kits to these stations. The kits, which included syringes and recently donated blood, saved lives. However, the kits were not widely available. Two problems limited their use: getting blood to the doctors and obtaining enough blood to meet the massive demand.

MEDICAL CARE IN SPAIN

Spain seemed unlikely as the place where these problems could be solved. Health care in Spain was somewhat behind the times. The hospitals, like the schools, were operated by the Catholic

Church, and the nuns who provided bedside care were not trained as nurses. Spain had not participated in World War I, so the innovations that conflict brought to Europe did not reach Spain. The doctors did not have access to the latest medical knowledge; they were not even scrubbing down before or between surgeries or wearing gloves. The number of health-care professionals and the level of expertise may have been adequate in peacetime, but the many casualties of the Spanish Civil War quickly overwhelmed the country's resources.

Enter the International Brigades. Of the thousands of volunteers from foreign countries who rallied to the cause of the Spanish Republic, a few hundred were surgeons, physicians, nurses, and medical technicians. They cleaned the hospitals and introduced sanitary practices. The citizens, angry at the Catholic Church, drove the nuns out and took their places. The foreign volunteers taught the local women how to care for the wounded and showed the Spanish doctors the newest medical practices. The international medical brigades set up field hospitals as close to the front as they could: in farmhouses, country clubs, ski resorts, and caves. They converted large vans into mobile hospitals.

The Spanish Civil War had several fronts at the same time. As the conflict grew bigger and more brutal, the need for blood in the many field hospitals was tremendous. The brigade doctors were up to date on the latest technology for transfusions. They just needed blood—lots of it. Within a few months of the start of the war, they had it, delivered by mobile blood transfusion services.

A NEW IDEA: MOBILE BLOOD TRANSFUSION SERVICE

Two doctors' names have been associated with the transfusion services. The Canadian Norman Bethune, who established a system in Madrid for delivering blood in December 1936, is sometimes credited with this innovation. However, the Spaniard Frederic Durán-Jordà was already operating a mobile service in Barcelona four months before Bethune began his.

Before the war began, Durán-Jordà, a medical doctor, directed a hospital laboratory. He had performed a few transfusions, all direct transfusions. However, he kept up with advances in medicine, so he knew about experiments in other countries with indirect blood transfusion.

When the war started, Durán-Jordà was put in charge of finding a way to get blood to the battlefield. He and his team got to work improving the infant process of indirect blood transfusion.

Durán-Jordà developed a new system for filtering blood and designed a special sealed glass container that kept the blood free from air and contaminants. He reduced the possibility of adverse reactions by mixing blood of the same type from six donors. He confirmed that adding sodium citrate to the blood kept it from clotting. Within weeks, he had a system by which blood could be collected and preserved, stored under refrigeration for eighteen days without losing any quality, transported without damage, warmed in water for twenty minutes, and infused into an injured person by only two technicians. As important as these technical

Frederic Durán-Jordà (1905–1957)

Dr. Durán-Jordà had no trouble relating to the men whose lives he saved. He grew up among them, in the Catalan capital of Barcelona. He was raised in the working-class district of the city, where his father operated a wine shop. Durán-Jordà had an advantage many of his friends did not; he had an education. In the early 1900s, few children in Spain went to school beyond the age of twelve. But Durán-Jordà's teachers, recognizing his brilliance, prodded his father to send him to secondary school and college, where he earned a degree in medicine.

Durán-Jordà, interested in the chemical aspects of medicine, began his medical career in the Hospital Clinic of Barcelona, not in patient care but in laboratory analysis. He published his observations and discoveries in two books and a number of articles in professional journals.

Durán-Jordà was concerned about the health of his countrymen. He gave free public lectures on first aid and other health-care topics so the common people could improve their lives. He advocated for a national health-care system in which doctors received salaries so they could treat everyone regardless of ability to pay. His development of the Barcelona Blood Transfusion Service was prompted by the desperate need of so many Spaniards.

However, when Franco's forces closed in on Barcelona, Durán-Jordà knew his kindness would not be rewarded. He fled Spain and was granted refuge in England. There, he helped set up a British blood transfusion system that saved many soldiers in World War II. After the war, he worked in Manchester, England, where he died of leukemia at age fifty-one.

innovations were, Dr. Durán-Jordà's revolutionary contribution to medicine was not only his treatment of blood; it was also his organization of a system for collection, storage, and delivery of that blood.

COLLECTING THE BLOOD

To supply the life-saving fluid, Durán-Jordà depended on the patriotism of the citizens of Barcelona. He recruited his first donors through announcements over the radio and at concerts and other public events. Before long, he had a list of 14,000 volunteers; by the end of the war, that number had risen to 28,900. A file was made for each one noting the blood type and listing each time the person gave blood. The blood was tested for malaria and other diseases.

Donors were organized according to the places where they worked or clubs to which they belonged. Every workplace and club had a *responsible,* a person who assumed responsibility for getting specific donors to the hospital when their blood was needed. Since the blood was good for just eighteen days, donors were called only when a battle seemed imminent. Durán-Jordà estimated how much blood was likely to be needed, telephoned the responsibles, and gave them the names of the volunteers he wanted. He took care that no one gave more frequently than every three weeks. His team could collect 100 to 130 pints (50 to 60 liters) from 150 donors in two hours. In an article he wrote after the war, Durán-Jordà said, "In 2 ½ years of work, we never at any time failed to obtain donors."

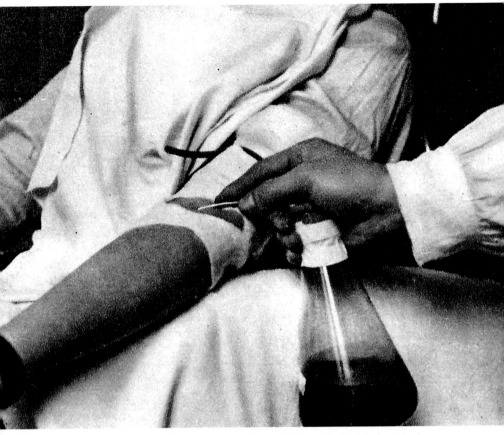

Blood collection in Barcelona was efficient. One technician placed a tourniquet on the donor's arm, another swabbed the arm with iodine, and another inserted the needle to withdraw the blood.

GETTING THE BLOOD TO THE FRONT

Some of those donors had type O blood, then thought to be the universal donor. (It was later determined that only type O– was universal; O+ could be transferred to some but not all types.) This blood was sent to field hospitals. On the field, doctors had no time to test a wounded person's blood, so everyone who received a transfusion in a field hospital was given type O. The other blood went to hospitals farther from the battle action, where less serious cases were treated. Everything about the collection, transport, and transfusion of the blood was carefully documented. The tubes of blood were refrigerated and delivered in thickly insulated boxes. The first vehicle Durán-Jordà was able to obtain to ship his precious cargo was a refrigerated truck used to haul fish. It was perfect!

In its two and a half years of operation, the Barcelona Blood Transfusion Service delivered more than 19,000 pints (8,990 L) of blood, more than twenty-seven thousand tubes. Dr. Bethune's similar transfusion service in Madrid supplied even more. The system that gave doctors at the battlefront a ready supply of blood for immediate transfusion was an innovation that possibly saved the lives of more injured soldiers than any other practice. It was adopted by every Western nation and used extensively in World War II and every major conflict since.

Hermann Göring, a fighter pilot ace in World War I, downed twenty-two enemy planes and was awarded two Iron Crosses along with other medals.

Test Results

The Spanish Civil War was a rare opportunity for Germany. Whether Hermann Göring intentionally used the event to test new planes and new tactics as he claimed or the testing just happened, the war was an ideal incubator for aeronautical innovation. The Condor Legion was a fairly small force, so any new idea traveled quickly, and the ones that worked were adopted by everyone. The men who volunteered for service in Spain were young and adventuresome, even daring; they were eager to propose and try things that had not been done before. The command structure was somewhat informal, so junior officers were not afraid to make suggestions. The commanders were hands-on, flying missions themselves; they understood the effects and recognized the value of the new tactics they tried.

Because they were far removed from their superiors in Germany, they were free to make changes and implement new ideas without interference.

The war fostered aerial combat innovation also because it was a real-life experience that carried little risk for the Germans. The Luftwaffe pilots could test a few planes, uncover their weaknesses in actual air fights, and correct their flaws. They could experiment with different formations and maneuvers against an inferior air force. The most they stood to lose if their innovations were flops were a handful of planes and a few men. If they failed completely, it would be the Nationalists in Spain who would suffer, not the Nazis in Germany. Göring was quite free to test his young Luftwaffe and come up with innovative methods and machines, but the results of the tests were not always interpreted correctly.

THE ROLE OF PLANES IN WARFARE

In a major test, the Spanish Civil War permitted the Luftwaffe to examine conflicting theories regarding the best military use of aircraft. Following the advent of air power in World War I, two schools of thought had developed regarding the role of planes in warfare: strategic or tactical.

The strategic approach is the use of air power, specifically bombs, to destroy a country's ability to wage war. It targets factories that produce armaments, farms that feed the fighters, and transportation networks that bring supplies to the front. It is conducted away from the field of combat, in a country's industrial centers or in cities. Therefore, it affects civilians as well as soldiers. The idea behind the strategic approach is that it cripples the enemy's economy, wears away the people's will to fight, and thus drives leaders to surrender.

The tactical approach is the use of aircraft in battle. It targets armies and their equipment in or in preparation for specific engagements. Tactical air power in the 1920s and 1930s was simply ground support—that is, the planes were used to support military forces on the ground, to help soldiers win battles. Their bombs were used to annihilate the enemy's air force, tanks, and armored cars; disrupt its communication; cut off its supplies; and demoralize its soldiers. Basically, the planes cleared the way for ground units to attack.

The debate over which was the more effective role for aircraft in war began almost as soon as planes demonstrated their potential in World War I. Three influential airmen advocated for the strategic approach: the Italian Giulio Douhet, the Englishman Hugh Trenchard, and the American Billy Mitchell. All three agreed that planes had a tactical role, but they argued that the strategic role was more important. They believed that strategic bombing would shorten conflicts and thus result in fewer deaths. Douhet went so far as to suggest that aircraft alone could win wars; armies and navies would become irrelevant.

The reason the debate mattered is that the two approaches demanded two different types of planes. Strategic use required heavy bombers—large, long-range aircraft that could carry massive amounts of explosives. Heavy bombers were needed to inflict the large-scale damage of strategic missions. Smaller tactical planes were medium bombers; they carried smaller **payloads** sufficient to achieve the more precise objectives of the battlefield. As it built its secret air force, the Luftwaffe had to decide how many of each type of aircraft to produce, and that determination depended on whether the emphasis would be on strategic or tactical bombing.

THEORIES TESTED IN SPAIN

The German air force began with a balanced approach. Walther Wever, chief of staff of the Luftwaffe, saw the value of both medium and heavy bombers, of tactical and strategic warfare. To add to his fleet of smaller planes, he ordered heavy, four-engine bombers from Junkers and Dornier. These planes were still in the design stage when Wever was killed in a plane crash in 1936, two weeks before the start of the uprising in Spain. Göring canceled the orders for the strategic aircraft. He reasoned that the factories could produce five smaller, twin-engine bombers for every two of the four-engine bombers. Still, several in the high command continued to argue for the big bombers. It would be up to the Condor Legion to test the two theories in actual combat and demonstrate which was preferable: tactical or strategic use of air power.

The strategic approach did not seem particularly appropriate in Spain. The country's economy was largely agricultural, so there was not much industry to bomb. The two attempts at intimidating the population by attacking cities, the terror bombings of Madrid and Guernica, failed. But most of the tactical missions were easy successes. Condor Legion Field Commander Wolfram von Richthofen, cousin of the Red Baron of World War I fame, informed the Luftwaffe leaders that the German air force, not the Nationalist Army, was responsible for the military victories. The planes, he insisted, carried the main thrust of the battle. Richthofen praised the virtues of the Stuka and argued convincingly for the tactical use of air power.

THE DEBATE SETTLED

The legion saw the difference air power made in battle when an Italian force of fifty thousand soldiers, fighting on the Nationalist side, launched an attack on the city of Guadalajara. The assault began in typical fashion, with a barrage of artillery fire on the Republican positions from the ground and the air. After four days of relentless attacks, the Republican defenders fell back; air power was on the Nationalist side, winning the battle.

However, as the Italian column slogged its way toward Guadalajara, heavy rain and sleet drenched the roads and shrouded the combatants in thick fog. When the Republicans mounted a counteroffensive, the Italian planes, based in fields far to the north, were mired in the mud of their rain-soaked airstrips, unable to taxi for takeoff. The few pilots who managed to get into the air had to turn back because they could not see through the low clouds and dense fog. At that point, the Nationalist soldiers had almost no air support. The planes of the Republicans, on the other hand, were housed in airports. These fighters and bombers roared from their cement runways unopposed, blew up the insurgents' tanks, and sent their soldiers scurrying in defeat. The arrival of the aircraft enabled the outnumbered Republican troops to hold their city, and the lack of air cover for the Italians was the main reason for their loss.

The Battle of Guadalajara, the first major defeat for Franco, convinced the German commanders that air power was vital to military success. It showed them that establishing and maintaining air superiority was essential to progress on the ground. It also demonstrated the importance of close communication between the army on the ground and the pilots in the air. In every major Nationalist offensive afterward, planes formed the first line of attack, as flying artillery supporting infantry action on the ground. The typical battle in the Spanish Civil War began with ground artillery or fighter planes attempting to take out the enemy's defenses, especially their antiaircraft weapons. Then medium bombers descended, protected by fighter aircraft, and dropped their loads. If the bombers were successful, soldiers marched in after them and sealed the victory. The success of this strategy, coupled with the failure of the terror bombings of Madrid and Guernica to break the will of the people, led Luftwaffe leaders to conclude that using planes as tactical support of ground fighting was the way to win wars.

APPLYING THE RESULTS

That conclusion led directly to decisions regarding what kinds of planes the German factories would produce. The first requests

Pablo Picasso's painting *Guernica* is an emotional portrayal of the pain and horrors of war.

were for medium bombers. The main ones provided were the Heinkel 111 and the Dornier 17, nicknamed the Flying Pencil. With the adoption of the Rotte and Schwarm enabling fighter planes to attack targets on the ground with relative ease, another idea emerged. Luftwaffe commanders reasoned that if fighter planes could be fitted with bombing capabilities, there would be no need for separate bombers and fighters. Thus the all-in-one fighter-bomber was created.

The favorite all-in-one was the single-engine Messerschmitt Bf 109. It was truly multipurpose, used for fighting, bombing, escort, reconnaissance, and ground attack. Spain was the testing ground that spawned several variants. Counting all its versions, more Bf 109s were manufactured than any fighter plane in history. From 1936 to 1945, a total of 33,984 were placed in service. In

Terror on Display

The 1937 World's Fair was held in Paris. The Soviet exhibit featured a sculpture of a worker and a peasant with hammer and sickle, and the German entry was topped with a giant swastika. Spain, a year into the civil war, wanted its pavilion to reflect the Republicans' defiant struggle against Francisco Franco. The organizers of the Spanish exhibit asked the country's most famous artist, Pablo Picasso, to create a painting that would expose and denounce Franco for his atrocities in Spain. Picasso accepted the assignment unenthusiastically. He was more interested in art than in politics or propaganda, and he had been living in Paris, completely untouched by the turmoil and misery in his homeland.

But his reluctance turned to anger when he read news reports of Franco's bombing of the Basque town of Guernica. He abandoned his original ideas and within six weeks had created a massive work of art. Titled simply *Guernica*, the black, white, and grey painting was in the unique style Picasso had introduced, cubism. It had no pictures of blood or combat, yet the misshapen figures in obvious agony clearly depicted the horrors of the bombing. Picasso declined to explain the images, but the brutality and suffering are unmistakable. The painting has come to symbolize not only Spain's fight but the anguish and inhumanity of war.

When the World's Fair closed, the canvas was displayed in several cities in Europe and America. Picasso refused to allow it to be in Spain as long as Franco remained in power. Today it is in a national art gallery in Madrid.

The Dornier 17, originally built to carry mail, was redesigned for military purposes with four machine guns (eight in later models).

World War II, the Bf 109 fought in every German campaign from the initial attack on Poland to the battles in the Soviet Union. Afterward, other countries continued to fly the versatile plane as late as the 1960s.

Another superstar tested in the Spanish Civil War was the Ju-87, the Stuka. Its performance was so impressive the Luftwaffe made precision bombing its foremost offensive strategy and the dive bomber its primary ground-attack plane. Nearly all bombers produced after the Stuka were required to have dive-bombing capability. Like the Messerschmitts, the Stuka was also a standout in World War II. In Stukas, Luftwaffe ace Hans-Ulrich Rudel destroyed three Allied warships, 519 tanks, at least 800 other armored vehicles, 4 trains, and numerous bridges and artillery pieces. By the end of the war, Germany had manufactured 6,500 Stukas and inspired other countries to develop dive bombers.

Because of its commitment to the tactical rather than strategic use of air power, the Luftwaffe did not build even one heavy bomber. However, its medium bombers were able to inflict major damage on civilian populations. The Condor Legion demonstrated their power to terrorize in Madrid and Guernica. Although those bombings had not yielded the desired results, they did teach the pilots how to use their aircraft to terrorize cities into surrender. They used that training a few years later when their planes flew over Warsaw, Rotterdam, and London, specifically targeting civilians.

MEDICAL ADVANCES

The innovations in military aviation from the Spanish Civil War were significant for warfare, but the medical innovations impacted the entire society. The changes that brought blood to frontline hospitals had effects that rippled through both Europe and America. The innovations that transformed the delivery of medical care were of two types: the treatment of blood and the organization of a system that ensured a ready supply of blood to meet both normal and emergency needs.

Just as the war gave the Luftwaffe a place to experiment with its planes and air combat strategies, it also gave doctors subjects upon whom they could test their scientific theories. Under ordinary circumstances, medical procedures would not be approved for general use until after much rigid research, but war was not an ordinary circumstance. Using an unproven procedure risked problems and even death, but in wartime, not doing anything often meant certain death. So doctors were willing to try practices that were still controversial.

In the Spanish Civil War, those practices included widespread use of indirect blood transfusion, Dr. Durán-Jordà innovative container that permitted sterile administration, the addition of chemicals to the blood to prevent clotting, and mixing blood from several donors. All these innovations proved effective and great improvements over what was then being done in civilian hospitals. Discoveries in military medicine are sometimes forgotten when the pressures of war are over, but these innovations were not lost. One of the reasons is that as the Spanish Civil War was coming to an end, people sensed that another crisis was looming. Some had the foresight to prepare for it. Another reason is that the transfusion services operated in both the military and civilian spheres, making the transition from wartime to peacetime practice easy.

At the close of the Spanish Civil War, Dr. Durán-Jordà published an article in *Lancet*, a British medical journal, describing the workings of the Barcelona Blood Transfusion Service in detail. He explained how he extracted, typed, treated, mixed, preserved, transported, and infused blood in great quantities. The information was available to physicians throughout the Western world. In his article, Durán-Jordà said the key to the success of his program was the recruitment and organization of donors

In addition to collecting blood for the wounded overseas, the American Red Cross used posters such as this to raise $146 million in 1943 for war relief.

in large cities. Anticipating what would become World War II, Great Britain established a transfusion service for the military with four collection centers around London. A doctor in France adopted Durán-Jordà's techniques in his transfusion service in Paris. Doctors in the United States organized the Blood for Britain project and found donors in New York City. Throughout the six-year war, banks of donors supplied massive amounts of blood not only to the front but also to the hospitals that treated civilians wounded in the aerial bombardments of major cities. Thus, some of the medical innovations of the Spanish Civil War, specifically basic techniques of indirect blood transfusion and the organization of donor bases, became firmly embedded in the general society. They have, of course, been improved upon, but they are still in use today.

A Stuka over France in 1940. The cross is the insignia of the German armed forces, including the Luftwaffe, and the swastika on the tail is the emblem of Hitler's Nazi Party.

CHAPTER SEVEN

Legacy of the War

As with any series of innovations, applications of the technological advances of the Spanish Civil War had mixed results. All were useful for at least some time beyond their original application, and some were stepping stones to greater innovations. Some were abandoned relatively quickly, and at least one continues today virtually unchanged. The future value of the new aerial combat tactics was decided in World War II.

The Spanish Civil War was the Luftwaffe's preparation for World War II. Because of that preparation, Germany entered the conflict with large, modern aircraft and well-trained pilots. The pilots had learned in Spain a number of principles about using planes in warfare. First, planes should be used as tactical weapons, providing close support for ground operations. Second, the first order of business in combat is to establish air superiority. Third, fighter planes perform best when arranged in Rotte and Schwarm formations. Fourth, dive bombing is the most accurate and most effective type of bombing. Finally, terror bombing of civilian populations should be avoided because it increases rather than decreases resistance. Air force commanders were eager to put what they had learned in Spain into practice in a bigger theater.

WORLD WAR II

They had their first chance on September 1, 1939, when Hitler launched World War II with an invasion of Poland. The operation began with an aerial assault on the country's airfields. The Luftwaffe destroyed Poland's aircraft and gained mastery of the skies. Then it went after its artillery, its ground troops, and routes that could supply reinforcements. Swarms of Stukas dove, one after the other, and dropped their bombs with piercing screams and deadly accuracy. Lastly, tanks and soldiers appeared, and Poland surrendered. This type of rapid-fire attack that combined air power, motorized vehicles, and infantry came to be known as blitzkrieg, or "lightning war." "Lightning" referred to the speed of the attack more than the suddenness. It had been tested in Spain and it worked in Poland.

It worked also in Denmark and Norway. Denmark surrendered within hours, and Norway gave in the day after the first plane appeared. The blitzkrieg was successful against the Netherlands, Belgium, and France. The tactics refined in Spain had proven effective, but all the countries Germany defeated had limited air power. The Luftwaffe was able to achieve air superiority fairly easily, as it had in Spain, and thus its planes were able to operate without significant opposition. Would the same tactics be effective against a large, powerful air force? Hermann Göring would find out when Hitler sent his Luftwaffe against Great Britain.

THE BATTLE OF BRITAIN

Hitler had hoped he would not have to fight Britain. He assumed British leaders would be so frightened by his spectacular blitzkrieg successes that England would stay out of his way. After France fell, Hitler tried to get England to sign a peace agreement, but British prime minister Winston Churchill rejected Germany's terms, rallying people to what he expected would be the Battle of Britain. That battle was launched on July 10, 1940. The heavy fighting lasted until the end of October.

The offensive proceeded according to the principles Germany had learned in Spain and that had been confirmed in the first engagements of the war. The first step was to gain air superiority. A land and sea invasion of England, called Operation Sea Lion, was on the drawing board, but the Luftwaffe would go first, without the other forces. It would knock out Britain's air bases, aircraft factories, radar stations, and other air defenses. Hitler hoped the air campaign alone would be sufficient to make Britain surrender.

However, the campaign did not go as expected. England's Royal Air Force was large and modern, and its pilots were well trained. British planes—Hurricanes and Spitfires—fought the German Bf 109s on fairly equal terms. They shot down many of the

Luftwaffe's Stukas because they could maneuver more easily than the slow bombers. The German bombers could deliver only a small payload on each flight because of their limited range and bomb capacity. The decision made during the Spanish Civil War to produce only medium bombers instead of heavy ones turned out to be a poor one.

The absence of heavy bombers was felt especially strongly in the middle of the Battle of Britain, when Germany switched its focus from tactical to strategic bombing. Germany had rejected the idea of strategic bombing but resorted to it in England somewhat by accident. A few German bombs had fallen on civilian areas of London, probably unintentionally. In retaliation, the Royal Air Force sent its bombers to Berlin. Furious, Hitler ordered his planes to run bombing raids over London. In what became known as the Blitz, London was bombed for fifty-seven nights in a row. London and other British cities continued to be bombed for several more months. Still England did not surrender. The Blitz confirmed one of the lessons Germany had learned in Spain: terror bombing of civilian populations hardens resistance.

Opposite: Failing to build heavy bombers, Germany developed the V-2 ground-launched rocket. One destroyed the Farringdon Market in London in 1945, killing 380 people.

Strategic Inventions of the Spanish Civil War

INNOVATIONS DISCARDED, INNOVATIONS RETAINED

The Battle of Britain was a turning point in World War II. The battle, fought entirely in the air, was also the point at which some of the innovative thinking of the Spanish Civil War was abandoned. No longer could Göring claim that the air force would win wars almost by itself. Precision bombing and other forms of tactical air combat were not necessarily more effective than the strategic bombing of an enemy's industrial bases. Small fighter-bombers and medium bombers were not enough. An air force also needed heavy bombers. Churchill recognized that fact, declaring in the middle of the battle, "The fighters are our salvation, but the bombers alone can provide the means to victory."

On the other hand, some of what had been learned in Spain was confirmed. Germany lost the Battle of Britain because its planes did not achieve air superiority. This failure reinforced the importance of air supremacy as a first goal for effective use of aircraft. The Rotte and Schwarm devised by Werner Mölders continued to be the best fighter formation. English pilots who had faced the formation in the Battle of Britain adopted it for their own units, calling it the finger-four formation. It eventually spread throughout the entire Royal Air Force. By the end of the war, the air forces of every major combatant were flying the finger-four. It remains a standard fighter formation today.

BLOOD AND BANKS

One successful innovation can spark a chain of new ideas. Such was the case with the blood transfusion services of the Spanish Civil War. The revolutionary concepts—indirect transfusion, banking supplies of blood, and maintaining an organized system of donors—made their way off the battlefields and into general medical practice. In the civilian hospitals, the processes of innovation were slower, but they rested on a solid foundation of knowledge acquired in the casualty clearing stations of the Spanish Republic. They were refined and improved in the ambulances and field hospitals of World War II. Because of a series of innovations beginning in the Spanish Civil War, people today who are seriously injured or who have certain medical conditions have ready access to blood or blood products that exactly meet their needs.

One of the first developments was the separation of blood into red and white cells, platelets, and plasma. This procedure meant a single donation of blood could benefit three people with different needs. A person with anemia might be given red blood cells, and a person with cancer might need platelets. Doctors quickly realized that infusion of plasma, the liquid part of blood, was often sufficient to treat blood loss in cases of major trauma. Plasma has the added benefit of not being affected by blood type; it can be given to anyone.

The next innovations were methods of freezing and drying plasma. Dried plasma can be stored without refrigeration, transported easily, and reconstituted with distilled water in minutes. Some emergency medical teams carry plasma transfusion kits. A host of other developments advanced the practice of transfusion. Methods of screening donated blood for diseases were developed. Fiberglass replaced gauze in filters for plasma transfusion. Plastic bags were introduced for collecting blood in 1951. Glass bottles were heavy, bulky, and breakable. They had to be sterilized and reused and carefully sealed. Plastic bags had lower risks of contamination and a number of other advantages.

All these innovations have enabled hospitals throughout the world to deliver blood safely and promptly when needed. According to the American Red Cross, someone in the United States needs blood every two minutes and nearly 21 million blood components are transfused each year. That blood comes from 6.8 million volunteer donors. Community blood banks and blood drives are the direct result of the innovations of the Barcelona and Madrid Blood Transfusion Services. Today, companies, schools, churches, and other community organizations conduct more than 145,000 blood drives yearly in the United States.

REWRITING THE LEGACY

It may seem somewhat ironic that the ability to deliver life-saving blood is a legacy of one of the bloodiest events of modern times. Today, both Spain and Germany are trying to make up for the atrocities and horror of the Spanish Civil War. The war ended with

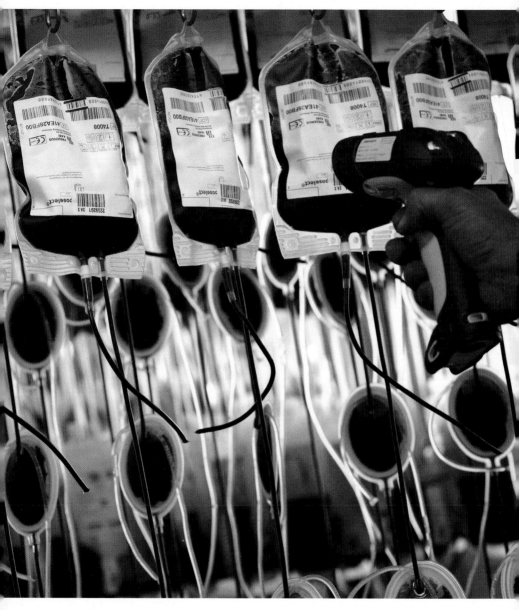

Most of the risks associated with blood transfusion come from the white cells in the blood. The whole blood in these bags in a Red Cross donation center in Germany is being filtered to remove the white cells.

Bloodless Surgery

As wonderful as the technology of blood transfusion is, the practice also has drawbacks. Obtaining and preparing the blood and blood products can be expensive, negative reactions can occur from receiving another person's blood, and transfusion carries a risk of infection. Today, some doctors are opting instead for a new technology called patient blood management. Instead of infusing stored blood or blood products into a patient undergoing surgery, doctors are finding ways of keeping and using the patient's own blood.

One method of blood management is interoperative blood salvage, which means saving the patient's blood during a surgery. Doctors and nurses collect the blood by suctioning the surgeon's cuts, and they put it back into the patient after the surgery. This technique is used when doctors expect a large volume of blood will be lost. In another form of blood management, the entire procedure is a closed system. The patient's blood is collected in bags and reintroduced into the patient at the end of the operation, but the bags always stay connected to the patient's body. It is kind of like adding a new loop to the circulatory system.

The main value of patient blood management is that patients never receive any blood but their own. Thus, they avoid the risks that come with conventional transfusion. It also eliminates the need for hospitals to acquire, test, type, treat, and store vast quantities of blood for normal use.

Spain firmly in the grip of Francisco Franco, the man responsible for the deaths of half a million of his countrymen. Franco kept that grip for thirty-six years, until his death in 1975. Part of his harsh control was a blackout on the truth of what happened during the war and under his leadership afterward. Today's Spaniards are repulsed and angered by Franco's actions. There is a movement to remove every symbol of his rule—statues, monuments, and names of streets and parks. Parliament passed a law in 2007 that barred such symbols from public places. All over Spain, they have been taken down.

Germany, too, wants to expunge the wrongs of the Hitler era. In 1997, the German parliament formally issued a belated apology to the citizens of Guernica for the Condor Legion's part in bombing the town. In 1998, Germany passed a law removing from military bases the names of all who had served with the Condor Legion. Apparently, people at the time did not remember that Werner Mölders, the World War II flying ace, had served in Spain. When his role in the Condor Legion came to light in 2005, Germany's defense minister scrubbed his name from a navy destroyer, an airbase, an army barracks, and a Luftwaffe fighter wing. Members of the air force's Mölders Squadron were told to take the armbands that bore his name off their uniforms. More than one hundred retired military officers sent a letter to newspapers protesting the government's action. However, the government was determined to repair its image, even at the cost of no longer considering an officer who had achieved great victories for his country a national hero.

On March 17, 2005, police supervised the removal of the last statue of Franco in Madrid, erected in 1959.

Strategic Inventions of the Spanish Civil War

Monuments in Spain to German pilots who died fighting for the Nationalist cause may soon suffer the same fate as the statues of Franco. Citizens argue over what should be done with three stone slabs that mark sites where airmen of the Condor Legion crashed in northern Spain. A monument in a Madrid cemetery to the memory of seven German pilots was vandalized in 2005 and 2012. Despite the attempts to rewrite a painful history, the events of the past remain true. Germany aided a ruthless rebellion, honorable men as well as brutal ones fought on both sides, and the war gave the world new technologies in aerial combat and life-saving medicine.

GLOSSARY

artillery Large-caliber guns such as cannons and missile launchers; also the military branch that specializes in using large-caliber guns.

authoritarian Refers to a form of government in which political power is concentrated in a leader or an elite group and others have little or no say.

clergy A member of a religious community; specifically, a priest or deacon.

coup An overthrow of a government; also called a coup d'etat.

democracy A government that serves the people.

elite Group that is or considers itself to be superior to others; often refers to the wealthiest and/or most powerful in society.

ideology Theory about how society, especially economics or politics, works or should work.

incendiary bomb An explosive designed to start a fire upon impact.

Luftwaffe Literally "air weapon," Luftwaffe was the name given to the air force of Germany from 1933 to 1946.

mutiny A revolt, usually of a ship's crew or other military against their officers.

parliamentary Relating to parliament.

payload Objects such as bombs carried by a plane for the purpose of fulfilling its mission.

prelude An event that precedes a larger or more important event.

reconnaissance Military exploration of enemy situations to gain information in preparation for attack or other action.

Rotte (plural *Rotten*) From the German word for "pair," a two-plane formation for fighter planes.

Schwarm From the German word for "flight," a four-plane air combat formation consisting of two Rotten.

sight A device that enables an airplane pilot or other person to locate a target and aim a bomb or other weapon at the target.

sovereign Having complete power or independence.

strafing Shooting at people quickly, repeatedly, and at close range from an airplane, usually with a machine gun.

throe A violent, painful spasm.

vic Flying formation in which three planes fly in the shape of the letter V.

BIBLIOGRAPHY

American Red Cross. "Blood Facts and Statistics." Retrieved July 1, 2016. http://www.redcrossblood.org/learn-about-blood/blood-facts-and-statistics.

Blinkhorn, Martin. *Democracy and Civil War in Spain: 1931-1939*. London, UK: Routledge, 1988.

Durán-Jordà, F. "The Barcelona Blood-Transfusion Service." *Lancet*, April 1, 1939. doi:10.1016/S0140-6736(00)60392-6.

Hendricks, Charles. "The Impact of the 'Disaster' of 1898 on the Spanish Army." Paper delivered at the 1998 Conference of Army Historians, Bethesda, MD, 1998. Retrieved May 26, 2016. http://www.history.army.mil/documents/spanam/ws-sparmy.htm.

Kacha, Peter. "Werner 'Vati' Mölders." Aces of the Luftwaffe. Retrieved June 12, 2010. http://www.luftwaffe.cz/molders.html.

Kendrick, Douglas B. *Medical Department United States Army in World War II: Blood Program in World War II*. Washington, DC: US Government Printing Office, 1964.

Kenwood, Alun. "Manifesto by General Francisco Franco, 17 July 1936." In *The Spanish Civil War: A Cultural and Historical Reader*, edited by Jon Cowans, 56-58. Providence, RI: Berg Press, 1993. Retrieved June 10, 2016. https://teachwar.wordpress.com/resources/war-justifications-archive/spanish-civil-war-1936/#manifesto.

Lowry, Carolyn S. "At What Cost? Spanish Neutrality in the First World War." Master's thesis, University of South Florida, 2009. Retrieved May 26, 2016. http://scholarcommons.usf.edu/cgi/viewcontent. cgi?article=3071&context=etd.

Lozano, Miguel, and Joan Cid. "Frederic Duran-Jorda: A Transfusion Medicine Pioneer." *Transfusion Medicine Reviews* 21, no. 1 (2007): 75–81. doi:10.1016/j.tmrv.2006.08.004.

Nevin, David. *Architects of Air Power*. Alexandria, VA: Time-Life, 1981.

Oh-Barcelona. "The Revolution of La Semana Tragica: When Barcelona Burned." 2010. Retrieved June 1, 2016. http://www.oh-barcelona. com/en/blog/2010/culture/history-culture/tragic-week-barcelona-3391.

Oppenheimer, Peter H. "From the Spanish Civil War to the Fall of France: Luftwaffe Lessons Learned and Applied." *Journal of Historical Review* 7, no. 2 (1986): 133–174. Retrieved May 26, 2016. http:// www.ihr.org/jhr/v07/v07p133_Oppenheimer.html#ftn54.

Rhodes, Richard. *Hell and Good Company: The Spanish Civil War and the War It Made*. New York: Simon and Schuster, 2015.

Schneider, William H. "Blood Transfusion Between the Wars." *Journal of the History of Medicine* 58 (April 2003): 187–224.

Solsten, Eric, and Sandra W. Meditz, eds. *Spain: A Country Study*. 2nd ed. Washington, DC: Library of Congress, Federal Research Division, 1990.

FURTHER INFORMATION

Websites

Abraham Lincoln Brigade Archives

http://alba-valb.org

The website of this nonprofit educational organization offers key information about the Spanish Civil War and the Americans who fought in it, including educational resources, archives, and articles.

Aircraft of the Spanish Civil War

http://bioold.science.ku.dk/drnash/model/spain/index.html

Still under development, this website has pictures, names, and information on all the aircraft involved in the Spanish Civil War.

History.com

http://www.history.com

This website offers text, video, audio, photos, and interactives on a wide range of world history topics including the Spanish Civil War.

Spanish Civil War

http://spanish-civil-war.org

This website provides detailed information about the history and events of and surrounding the Spanish Civil War.

Videos

Pablo Picasso: Guernica (1937)

https://www.youtube.com/watch?v=PbLTE-ERzYO

This clip describes the background for Picasso's painting *Guernica* and analyzes it.

The Spanish Civil War

https://www.youtube.com/watch?v=81RhewkQbOk

This very comprehensive, six-part educational film includes news footage from the Spanish Civil War.

Spanish Civil War: A Three-Minute History

https://www.youtube.com/watch?v=4DD162YpuhU

This video gives a brief overview of the Spanish Civil War.

World War II in Colour: The Spanish Civil War

https://www.youtube.com/watch?v=TDvz_53bjP4

This video describes the Spanish Civil War from beginning to end.

INDEX

ABOUT THE AUTHOR

Ann Byers is a teacher, youth worker, writer, and editor. With a degree in history, Byers particularly enjoys researching and learning about people and events from the past and sharing that learning with young readers.